To

_____

From

_____

To David for his support and encouragement
And Rosemary and Livi, who reminded me how
important these stories are

P.L.

Text by Elena Pasquali
Illustrations copyright © 2014 Priscilla Lamont
This edition copyright © 2014 Lion Hudson

The right of Priscilla Lamont to be identified as the illustrator of this work has been asserted
by her in accordance with the Copyright, Designs and Patents Act 1988.

Published by Lion Children's Books
an imprint of
Lion Hudson plc
Wilkinson House, Jordan Hill Road,
Oxford OX2 8DR, England
www.lionhudson.com/lionchildrens
ISBN 978 0 7459 6399 0
ISBN 978 0 7459 6547 5 (gift)

First edition 2014

Author Information
p. 8: Sarah Betts Rhodes (1824–1904)
p. 106: Walter J. Mathams (1851–1931)
p. 192: Lois Rock

Acknowledgments
Bible extracts are adapted from Good News Bible © 1994 published by the Bible Societies/
HarperCollins Publishers Ltd UK, Good News Bible© American Bible Society 1966, 1971,
1976, 1992. Used with permission.
The prayer by Lois Rock is copyright © Lion Hudson.

A catalogue record for this book is available from the British Library

Printed and bound in China, February 2014, LH25

The Lion
NURSERY
BIBLE

Retold by *Elena Pasquali*
Illustrated by *Priscilla Lamont*

LION
CHILDREN'S

CONTENTS

Old Testament

New Testament

7

Old Testament

God, who made the earth,
The air, the sky, the sea,
Who gave the light its birth,
Careth for me.

A CHILDREN'S HYMN

In the Beginning

For you, for me, for everyone, the world is our home.

But how did it begin? Why did it begin?

This story has been told and retold for more years than anyone can remember.

In the beginning there was nothing: just darkness and wildness… and God.

Then God spoke:
"Let there be light."
And the light shone.

In this way, God began to make the world.
"I want there to be sky," said God.
"Beneath its dome of blue, I want sea and land.

"I want plants of
every kind to unfold
their leaves. I want
bright flowers to
open, and their seeds
and fruits to ripen in
the sun.

"In the seas, let there be fish. May birds fly through the air and sing from the treetops.

14

"And let there be all kinds of animals –
the shy and the scampering;
the large and the lumbering;
the playful and the plodding:
each one different and special."

When all this was done, God made people.

"This world is your home," said God. "Please take care of all the good things I have made.

"Let every seventh day be a day of rest and enjoyment for everything in my creation.

"There is just one warning: one tree you must not touch.

"If you eat its fruit, bad things will happen."

Adam and Eve were happy in their paradise home.

Then, one day, Eve
heard a whisper… a
sneaky, snaky whisper.
"Did God really
tell you not to eat this
lovely fruit?

"How silly! It will make
you wise – as wise as God.

"Go on – try some."

Eve was tempted.
She picked some fruit
and took a bite.

"Adam!" she called. "Come and eat this.
It's delicious."

In this way, Adam and Eve
disobeyed their Maker. From that
moment, everything went wrong.
They had to work for
everything they needed.

There were
so many things
to worry about.

Worst of all, they had spoiled their friendship with God.

What a dreadful mistake they had made. Could it ever be put right?

NOAH AND THE ARK

Adam and Eve had children. Their children had children too… and so the years went by, and the world grew full of people.

But it was not a happy place: the people did nothing but argue and fight.

"I'm sorry I made them!" said God. "The only good person I can find is a farmer named Noah.

"I shall ask him to help me give the world a whole new start."

God told Noah the plan.

"I am going to send a flood. It will wash away the bad old world.

"You will build a boat: a huge ark that will float. You must take your family on it to keep them safe.

"You must also take a mother and a father of every kind of animal."

Noah set to work.

When the ark was ready, the animals and birds went on board and found a place to snuggle down. The people went on board and waited.

First God shut the door. Then God sent the rain.

The pitter pattering turned to splishing splashing.

Then the splishing splashing turned to swirling gurgling, as the rivers rose and water covered the land.

Soon there was nothing but the flood –
nothing except Noah and his ark…
and God.

For days and weeks the ark floated.

Even when the rain stopped,
the ark went on floating.

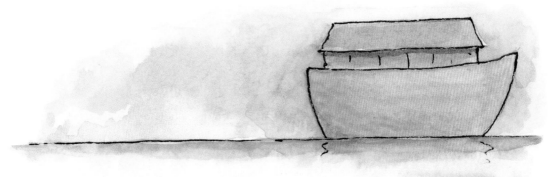

Then one day…

Crunch! The ark bumped into a mountaintop.
Little by little the flood went down.

Day by day more mountaintops appeared.
Noah sent out a raven to look for land, but it flew away.

Later, Noah sent out a dove.

It came back with an olive twig in its beak.

Somewhere the world was growing green again.

When at last the land was dry, God told Noah to bring everyone out of the ark.

"I want the animals to have young and fill the world again," said God.

"I want your family to have children and grandchildren. I want them to sow seeds and gather crops just as you used to.

"Look: there is my rainbow in the sky.
"It is the sign of my promise never to
flood the world again."

33

Abraham and His Family

Long, long ago lived a man named Abram.

It was so long ago that Abram knew the names of everyone in his family tree right back to Noah.

He was a wealthy man. He had sheep, goats, cattle, donkeys, and even camels.

He also had a beautiful wife named Sarai.
But he had no son. And that was the thing
that made Abram sad.

One day, God spoke to him, with the most astonishing news.

"Abram," said God. "I want you to leave your home and go to the land of Canaan.

"It is there that you will have a family. It will grow and grow.

"Your family will be my people. They will show the world what it means to live as my friends again. In this way they will bring my blessing to everyone."

Abram trusted God. He set out with Sarai and his entire household to begin a new life.

It was a big change. Abram left his house in the
city and set out with only a tent for shelter.

He and his household made the long journey
to Canaan, always seeking fresh grass for the
animals.

Even when they found a good place, they could never stay long.

But that wasn't all.

The worst thing was that still Abram and Sarai had no son.

One night, God spoke to Abram again.

"Come outside. Look up at the stars. There are far more than you can count.

"One day there will be more people in your family than there are stars in the sky."

Abram could only hope that God would keep his promise.

Other people in the household had children.

Sarai always felt sad when she saw them laughing and playing.

She was getting old. "Too old to be a mother," she sighed.

"I keep my promises," God told Abram. "From now on, you will be called Abraham, and the name means 'father of many'.

"Your wife will be Sarah, and the name means 'princess'."

Then, at long last, God's promise did come true. Abraham and Sarah had a baby boy.

Now at last they could be truly happy.

They named the child Isaac, and the word means "laughter".

Abraham was so proud to see his boy grow.
Now he could really trust in God's blessing.

JOSEPH AND HIS BROTHERS

Joseph was eager
to find out why
his father had
called him.

"This most wonderful coat," said Jacob, "is a
gift for you, my most wonderful son.

"My grandfather Abraham and my father
Isaac would be proud of you, and you are to be
the head of the family after me."

Joseph felt proud, too. "It's going to be like a dream I had," he told his family. "In my dream we were all out harvesting. My sheaf was the best, and your sheaves bowed down to it."

Joseph's ten elder brothers scowled. "We don't want to bow down to you," they sneered.

Not long after, the ten brothers were out looking after their father's flocks.

Jacob sent Joseph to check on them.
"Let's show him what we think of his boasting," they agreed. And they beat him up.

By chance, some traders were passing by.
"Let's sell Joseph as a slave,"
agreed the brothers.

And they did. They
ripped up the wonderful
coat and took bits of it
back to Jacob.
"We think wild
animals must
have eaten
him," they lied.

In faraway Egypt, Joseph
became a slave. He served
his master well. But his
master's wife told lies about
him and said he had tried to
harm her. For this, Joseph
was thrown into prison.

Still he tried to do his best. He made friends, too, because God had given him the wisdom to explain dreams.

One day, the king of Egypt had a puzzling dream. No one in the palace could explain its meaning. Someone sent for Joseph.

"In my dream," said the king, "were seven fat cows. Then seven thin cows came and ate them.

"Next I saw seven plump ears of grain. Seven thin ones came and ate them."

Joseph bowed and smiled. "I can explain," he said. "The dreams mean that there will be seven years of good harvests. Then will come seven years of bad harvests.

"You need someone to make sure everyone stores grain from the good years so there is food for the bad ones."

The king gave Joseph the job.

When the years of bad harvests came, Joseph alone was in charge of who could buy food.

One day, ten hungry men came from far away. They bowed low.

They were Joseph's elder brothers.

But where was his younger brother, Benjamin?

Without saying who he was, Joseph demanded that the men tell him all about their family.

He found out that Benjamin was still alive.

"Bring him here to prove your story!" he said.

When Benjamin arrived, Joseph made a plan to keep him.

He made it look as if Benjamin had stolen a silver goblet.

"He must stay here in prison," Joseph declared.

One of the ten stepped forward. "Please let Benjamin go back to our father," he pleaded. "Benjamin reminds him of a son he lost long ago. Keep me instead."

At last Joseph knew that his brothers were sorry. "I am Joseph!" he cried. "God has kept me safe so that I can keep you all safe now.

"Bring my father and all the family to live here in Egypt."

Moses and the King

The mother looked at her baby son and smiled.

"I have so many hopes and dreams for him," she said to her daughter, Miriam.

Then she sighed. "I wonder if any of them will come true.

"Long ago, a man named Joseph welcomed our people to Egypt.

"Now a different king has made us all slaves.

"He has told his soldiers to throw our baby boys in the river!"

"No!" said Miriam. "We won't let that happen!"

She and her mother cradled the baby boy in a special basket. Carefully they floated it in the river.

A princess of Egypt came along to bathe. She saw the basket, and found the baby.

"Oh, poor baby," she said. "I am going to keep him and name him Moses. But who will look after him for me?"

Miriam had been hiding close by. Now she stepped forward.

"I know someone who can help," she said. She fetched her mother.

Moses grew up as a prince in Egypt. He had
everything he could wish for. But he knew he
really belonged to the slave people,
who had nothing.

As a young man,
he tried to help
them. But that got
him into trouble, and
he had to run away.

In the wild country, he became a shepherd. One day he saw a bush, covered in flames but not burning.

He heard God speaking:

"Moses, I have chosen you to go back to the king of Egypt. Tell him to let my people go free."

Moses was afraid, so God said he could ask his brother Aaron to help him. Together they went to ask the king to let the people go.

"No!" was the reply. The king didn't care about God. He only cared about keeping his slaves.

"I won't let them go!" he said.

"Then you will be disobeying God," said Moses. "That means trouble."

And there was trouble:

too many frogs,

too many flies,

great clouds of hungry locusts that ate the crops.

All kinds of things went wrong.

Then the Egyptians
started getting ill.
The troubles made
the king change
his mind.

"Take your people and go!" he told Moses.
So they went. The king changed his mind
again and sent soldiers to bring his slaves back.

It was too late.

God made a path through the sea, and the people walked to freedom.

DAVID AND GOLIATH

David waved his older brothers goodbye.

They were soldiers, going off to fight in the king's army.

"Why is there war?" David asked his father.

Jesse sighed.

"It's to do with this land of Canaan," he replied.

"We believe God wants it to be our home.

"Long ago, Moses brought our people here. On the way, he gave our people laws. He said that if we obeyed them then we would be God's people, and we would live here in safety.

"Now the Sea People – the Philistines – want to make the land theirs."

David had plenty of time to think about that.
He was the youngest in his family. He had to stay
at home in Bethlehem and look after the sheep.

"One day I'll be a fighter," he said, as he threw stones with his sling to get his aim just right.

"Already I can fight off bears – and lions."

One day, Jesse asked David to take a basket of food to his brothers. He found them lining up for battle.

As they waited, a soldier walked out from the enemy army: a giant of a man named Goliath. His weapons shone. His helmet glinted in the sunshine.

"Who dares fight me?" he cried. "Beat me, and you win the war!"

David's brothers and all the king's soldiers ran back to camp.

"No one has a chance against Goliath," David's brothers explained. "King Saul has offered a big reward to anyone who beats him. But who would dare?"

"I'll go," said David.

News of what he said reached King Saul. He asked to see the young fighter.

Then he saw David. "You're only a boy," he said. "You don't have a chance."

"God has helped me fight bears and lions," replied David. "God will help me win the battle for all our people."

David took just his stick and his sling. He stopped by a stream to pick up five stones. Then he walked toward Goliath.

"How dare you!" roared Goliath.
"I dare because God is with me!" cried David.
He slung a stone.
Goliath fell.

It was the first of many victories.

In the end, David became the next king.

He made Jerusalem his city.

"Here we will build a Temple," he told the people. "Here we will pray and sing to the God who helps us."

And he wrote this song:

"The Lord is my shepherd,
And I am his sheep:
My home – a green meadow
By pools clear and deep.

"I trust in my shepherd,
I've nothing to fear,
For God will stay close
And no danger come near."

Jonah and the
Deep Blue Sea

Jonah was in a hurry.

"Where can he be going?" people wondered.

"Oh – I know. He's one of God's messengers. He must be off to tell people what God wants them to know."

Indeed, God had told Jonah to go to Nineveh. "Tell the people to change their wicked ways before they are punished," God had said.

But Jonah was hurrying the other way. He got on a boat that was bound for far away.

Safe on board, Jonah smiled to himself. "Now the people of Nineveh will get the punishment they deserve," he chuckled.

Then a dreadful storm blew in. The waves crashed. The wind roared.

"Oh no!" said Jonah. "God is angry with me for disobeying him!

"You must throw me overboard," he told the sailors. "The storm is *my* punishment, not yours."

Into the sea he went.

Down, down, down sank Jonah: down to the darkest deep.

Suddenly a huge sea creature swallowed him up.

86

Deep inside its belly, Jonah understood.
"Help me, God!" he prayed. "Please help!
I'll do everything you ask if you save my life,
I promise."

The sea creature belched Jonah onto a beach.
Jonah hurried to Nineveh.

"Listen, everyone,"
he cried. "God is angry
about the wicked
things you do!
    "Change your ways
at once, or God will
send a disaster."

The people of Nineveh
looked worried.

So did the king. He was
very afraid of what might
happen. "Jonah is right,"
he said. "Everyone must
stop being bad right now
and start doing good."

So they
did. And God
forgave them.

No disaster came. Jonah went out of the city and built a little shelter just for himself.

"I can see you're very angry," said God.

"Of course I'm angry!" said Jonah. "The people of Nineveh deserved a punishment. You've just let them off.

"Anyway, it's too hot."

By way of answer, God woke a little seed next to the shelter. It grew in no time. Its leaves gave cool shade.

Jonah was delighted.

The next day, God sent a worm that chewed the plant, and it died.

The wind was hot. The leaves wilted.

Jonah was dismayed. "What a disaster!" he complained.

God spoke very, very quietly. "I see you feel very sad about your plant," said God. "I felt sad about the people of Nineveh. Even though they used to be bad, I always loved them."

DANIEL AND THE LIONS

When Daniel was a young man, everything seemed good.

He was wealthy. He was clever. He lived in the beautiful city of Jerusalem and said his prayers at the Temple there.

Then soldiers came from Babylon. They won a fierce battle. They marched their prisoners to Babylon, Daniel among them.

"I can still live as God would like,"
said Daniel to himself. "In my
prayers, I shall ask God to
help me do what is good
and right."

First one king, then the next, and the next
noticed that Daniel was wise. The time came when
King Darius gave Daniel a very important job.
That made other people very jealous.

They whispered
together. They made
a plan. They went to
see Darius.

"O king," they said, bowing low.
"You alone are great and wonderful.
"No one in heaven or on earth is
greater. Anyone who thinks
there is someone greater
should be punished."

"How true!" said the king.

"They should be thrown to the lions!" said the men.

"What a very good idea," said the king. "I'll make that the law."

The men chuckled. They went to find Daniel. They knew what they would see.

He was at his window, saying prayers to God.

They grabbed him roughly and dragged him to the king.

"Daniel shows more respect for his God than for you!" they cried. "Throw him to the lions!"

King Darius was dismayed. "Oh, I can trust Daniel," he protested.

"But you cannot break your own law," replied the men.

Indeed, the king could
not. Daniel was thrown
into a pit of lions.

Their claws were long. Their teeth
were sharp. Their mouths were huge.
But Daniel knelt quietly and said
his prayers.

God sent an angel to stop the lions eating him.

The next day, King Darius hurried to the pit. He hardly dared look. Was there any hope Daniel was alive?

"Are you still there?" he called.

"I am," replied Daniel. "God has kept me safe."

Then even King Darius understood. "Daniel's God is greater and more wonderful than anyone else on earth or in heaven," he declared.

New Testament

Jesus, friend of little children,
Be a friend to me;
Take my hand, and ever keep me
Close to thee.

A CHILDREN'S HYMN

Jesus is Born

The angel spoke very gently.
"Please don't be afraid, Mary.
I bring a message from God."
Mary listened, wide-eyed in
astonishment. Had an angel
really come to Nazareth to
see her?

"God has chosen you to be the mother of his Son," said the angel. "You will name him Jesus. He will be a king – the one who welcomes people into God's own kingdom."

Mary thought hard. "I will do as God wants," she said.

When Joseph heard that Mary was expecting a baby, he was sad. "It's not my baby," he sighed, "so I don't think Mary and I will be getting married now."

Then, in a dream, an angel spoke to him.

"God has chosen you to take care of Mary and her baby," said the angel.

When Joseph woke up, he went to find Mary.

"You know I was planning a journey to my home town of Bethlehem," he said, "to put my name on a list the emperor wants."

Mary nodded.

"We will go there as family," he said.

When they arrived,
the town was crowded.
The only room for
Mary and Joseph was
a stable. There, Mary's
baby was born.

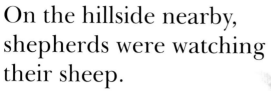

On the hillside nearby,
shepherds were watching
their sheep.

An angel appeared.

"I have wonderful news!"
cried the angel. "God's Son has
been born in Bethlehem.

"You will find him wrapped
up snugly and lying in a manger."

For one glorious golden moment, the sky
was filled with singing. Then the sky went
dark again.

"Can it be true? We must go and see,"
agreed the shepherds.

They found Mary and her baby just as the angel had said.

And they told Mary of all they had seen.

All the while, a star
was shining high above.
Wise men from far
away were following the
path on which it shone.

"We believe it
will lead us to a
newborn king,"
they said.

It led them to Jesus.

They gave him rich gifts:
gold, frankincense, and myrrh.

Joseph watched the men as they set out for home.

"Now we, too, must travel on," he said to Mary. "We must keep Jesus safe, so he can grow up to do all the things that God has chosen him for."

JESUS GROWS UP

Jesus grew up in
Nazareth.

He learned from
Joseph how to be a
carpenter.

He went to school like the other boys.
He learned to read the stories of his people.
He learned about their faith in God.

He learned their
wise teachings and
remembered them.

When he was a young man,
he became a preacher.

He wanted to tell people
about God's love.

He chose twelve friends to
help him, among them four
fishermen who worked on
Lake Galilee. Their names
were Peter and Andrew,
James and John.

"Leave your nets and follow me," he told them. "You won't be catching fish anymore. Instead, you will be gathering people into God's kingdom of love."

Crowds gathered to listen
to what he had to say.

"Make it your aim to live as
God wants," Jesus told them.

"Go out of your way
to be kind to others.

"Don't show your love only to your friends: show your love to all people, even to those who are unkind, and do good things to help them.

"When you pray, say these words:

'Our Father in heaven,
May everyone respect your holy name.
May your kingdom come.
May your will be done,
On earth, as it is in heaven.

Give us this day our daily bread.
Forgive us our wrongdoing,
As we forgive those who do wrong to us.
Protect us from those things that would
lead us astray,
And keep us safe.'

"Look around. God takes care of each tiny bird, each lovely flower.

"God will also take care of you.

"The kingdom of God is like a tree that has grown from a tiny seed. It is a place where many birds can nest and be safe.

"Everyone is welcome in God's kingdom."

LOST AND FOUND

Jesus welcomed all kinds of people. "Whatever you have done, you can be God's friends again," he told them.

This was good news for people who knew they had done wrong things.

It made others very angry. "We have always tried very hard to do what is right," they grumbled. "We're the kind of people whom God likes. Not that rabble over there."

Jesus told a story.

"There was once a man who had a hundred sheep. One day when he was counting them, he found he had only ninety-nine.

"What did he do?
"He left the ninety-nine safely
in the field and went looking.

"When at last he found his lost sheep, he was
overjoyed. He carried it gently home.

"'Let's have a party,' he called to his friends.
'I've found my lost sheep.'

"God is like that shepherd," said Jesus. "God is happy when even one person who has gone off the wrong way comes home to the kingdom."

Jesus told another story.

"There was once a man who had two sons. One worked hard on the farm. The other asked for his share of the family money and set off on his travels.

"He spent his money on all kinds of worthless things.

"He ended up penniless and hungry. The only job he could get was looking after pigs.

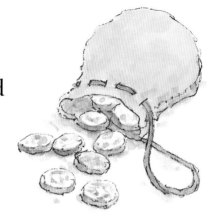

" 'What a mess I've made of everything,' he wept. 'The best I can do is to go back to my father and say sorry.'

"It was a long way home. His father saw him coming and ran to greet him.

" 'Welcome home!'
he cried. Then,
'Come on everyone,
let's have a party.'

"The hardworking son scowled at the news.

" 'We have to be glad,' said the father. 'We all thought your brother was lost. Now he has been found.' "

STORM AND SUNSHINE

Jesus preached in all the towns around Lake Galilee. He and his friends often went from place to place by boat.

On one journey, Jesus was so
tired that he fell asleep. Suddenly
a storm blew up. The wind
howled. The waves crashed.

"Help us!" cried the friends,
as they shook Jesus awake.
"Don't you care about what's happening?"

Jesus stood up in the boat. "Hush," he said to the storm. "Be still."

At once the lake was calm. The sky cleared.
The friends whispered among themselves.
"Who can Jesus be? Even the wind and waves
obey him."

They were still wondering some time later, when they arrived at a crowded shore.

People had heard that Jesus was coming, and they wanted to see him.

One man, whose name was Jairus, pushed his way to the front.

"Please come to my house," he begged. "My daughter is very ill. I'm hoping you can make her well."

"Of course I'll come," said Jesus, but it was slow going. There were just so many people trying to get near to Jesus.

And Jesus didn't seem to mind. He even stopped to talk to a woman, who simply touched his cloak.

"I haven't been well for years," she said to him. "I was hoping you could heal me."

"You will be well from now," replied Jesus.

Then a messenger arrived from Jairus's house. "I'm afraid it's too late," he whispered to Jairus. "Your daughter... I'm sorry... She's just died."

"It's not too late," said Jesus. He went to the house and waved aside a group of women who were already weeping noisily.

He went to the room where
Jairus's daughter lay still on
her bed.

"Little girl," he said gently,
"time to get up."

The girl sat up at once. Jairus
and his wife were overjoyed.

"There's no need
to say anything about
this," Jesus told them.
"Just look after your
little girl. I think she'll
be hungry!"

THE GOOD SAMARITAN

One day, a man came up to Jesus.

"We both do the same kind of work," he said, rather slyly. "I teach people about how to live as God wants, just as you do. And here's the question: what is the single most important thing that God wants?"

"You've read the holy books of our people," said Jesus. "What do they say?"

"Love God most of all," replied the man, "and treat others as you want to be treated."

"Quite right," said Jesus. "I thought you'd know the answer."

The man frowned. Had Jesus made him look foolish? He asked another question: "Who are these 'others'?"

Jesus told a story.

"There was once a man who was going from Jerusalem to Jericho.

"On that lonely road, bandits came and beat him up. They left him lying in the road.

"A priest from the Temple in Jerusalem came along. He saw the man and hurried on past on the far side of the road.

"Next, a helper from the Temple came along. He looked at the man. It was an upsetting sight – but what could he do?

"He simply hurried on by.

"Next, a Samaritan came by."

The teacher looked startled. What would
anyone expect of a Samaritan? They didn't pray
at the Temple! They didn't understand the holy
books like the priests did!

Jesus just went on with the story.
"The Samaritan stopped," he said.
"He cleaned the man's cuts
and bandaged them.

"Then he lifted the man onto his donkey and took him to an inn.

"The next day he had to travel on. 'Here is money,' he said to the innkeeper. 'Please take care of that poor man for me. If it costs more, I'll pay you the extra next time I come.'

"Now," said Jesus to the teacher, "which of the three treated the man as he himself would have liked to be treated?"

"The one who was kind to him," said the teacher.

"Quite right," said Jesus.
"Now you can go and do the same."

Jesus in Trouble

It was festival time in Jerusalem. The road to the city was crowded.

Then Jesus came along, riding on a donkey.

"This is exciting," the people whispered. "Perhaps Jesus will do something amazing right in the middle of the festival!

"He talks about a kingdom. Perhaps he'll make himself king!"

They began to cheer and to wave palm branches.

"Long live the king!" someone shouted.

Jesus went to the Temple. There was a market in the Temple square, with people selling all kinds of things for the festival.

"This is all wrong!" cried Jesus. "The Temple is meant to be the place where people come to say prayers – not to be sold things at silly prices."

He tipped up the market tables and sent everyone out.

The priests and the teachers frowned. "Jesus is nothing but trouble," they agreed. "We must get rid of him."

Jesus knew what they were thinking. He asked his friends to prepare a festival meal for them all to share.

Jesus broke the bread. "My body will soon be broken," he said.

He poured the wine. "My blood will soon be spilled," he said.

"When you share a meal like this, remember me.

"Remember all that I have told you about God's love. Remember to love one another."

The friends were puzzled at Jesus' words... except for Judas Iscariot, who slipped away.

After the meal, Jesus and his friends went to an olive grove, where they could sleep under the stars.

Jesus stayed awake, saying prayers.

"Dear Father God, I fear there are hard times ahead," he said. "If they must happen, please help me."

Just as he finished, Judas Iscariot arrived. He had made a wicked plan with the priests and the Temple teachers. He came with soldiers who led Jesus away.

They took him to the priests.

"Your teaching about God is all wrong!"
they told him. "You must be punished."

They took him to the Roman governor,
Pontius Pilate.
They said he was a troublemaker.
They arranged for Jesus to be put to death.

Jesus was crucified, nailed to a cross of wood. In the evening, just before the sun went down, friends came and took his body.

They laid it in a tomb
and rolled the stone door shut.
Jesus had brought them
hope and joy. Were those
things gone forever?

A New Beginning

It was early morning and the sky was pale. Some women were hurrying back to Jesus' tomb.

"We couldn't have come yesterday," they said. "It was the day of rest. This is our first and only chance to say a proper goodbye."

When they reached the tomb, they saw
the stone door had been rolled away.

Inside were two angels. "Jesus is not here," they said. "He is alive."

The women ran to tell Jesus' other friends.

Peter and John agreed to come and see,
but all they found was an empty tomb.

Only Mary from Magdala
stayed nearby. She saw a man.
"The gardener!" she thought.
"I'll ask him about Jesus' body."

When the man turned
to answer her question,
she saw.
It was Jesus. He really
was alive!

After that, Jesus appeared to his friends several times. They saw the marks of the nails on his hands and feet.

They listened as he told them what they must do next.

"Tell everyone the things I have told you," he said.

"Take care of those who are my followers, as a shepherd takes care of his sheep.

"I will soon go back to my Father in heaven," Jesus told them. "Do not be sad, for I will make a place ready there for you.

"One day soon God will give you the courage you need to speak out."

When the day came, Jesus' friends felt they were surrounded with wind and fire.

Boldly they went out into the world to tell everyone.

"Jesus is alive!" they said. "He came to show us all the way to live as God's friends; to welcome us into God's kingdom of love, God's heavenly paradise."

For blessings here
and those in store
we give thanks now
and evermore.